HENRI BERGSON

AN INTRODUCTION TO
METAPHYSICS

HENRI BERGSON

AN INTRODUCTION TO
METAPHYSICS

Translated by
T. E. HULME

Introduction by
THOMAS A. GOUDGE

Hackett Publishing Company
Indianapolis/Cambridge

English translation first published 1912

Reprinted by Hackett Publishing Company, Inc., 1999

Printed in the United States of America

05 04 03 02 01 00 99   1 2 3 4 5 6

For further information, please address
Hackett Publishing Company, Inc.
P.O. Box 44937
Indianapolis, IN 46244-0937

www.hackettpublishing.com

Library of Congress Cataloging-in-Publication Data

Bergson, Henri, 1859-1941.
    [Introduction à la métaphysique. English]
    An introduction to metaphysics / by Henri Bergson ; translated
by T. E. Hulme ; introduction by Thomas A. Goudge.
        p.   cm.
    Originally published: New York : Liberal Arts Press, 1949.
    Includes bibliographical references.
    ISBN 0-87220-475-8 (alk. paper). — ISBN 0-87220-474-X (pbk. :
alk. paper)
    1. Metaphysics.   I. Title.
B2430.B4I413   1999
110—dc21   99-28080
                                                            CIP

The paper used in this publication meets the minimum requirements
of American National Standards for Information Sciences—Perma-
nence of Paper for Printed Materials, ANSI Z39.48-1984.

∞

CONTENTS

NOTE ON THE TEXT

In a note dated Paris, October 18, 1912, Professor Henri Bergson authorized publication of the translation by Mr. T. E. Hulme. The statement reads, in English translation, as follows:

> I certify that the translation of my volume, *An Introduction to Metaphysics*, which has been prepared by Mr. T. E. Hulme, is the only English version to which I have given my authorization. I may add that Mr. Hulme was excellently well qualified for his task by the careful study that he has made of the whole series of my writings. I have examined his translation with care and am able to say that it renders with remarkable accuracy the thought and the conclusions presented in my volume.

The present edition follows Hulme's version except for spelling and punctuation, which have been revised throughout to conform to present-day American usage.

TRANSLATOR'S PREFACE

THIS CELEBRATED ESSAY was first published in the *Revue de Métaphysique et de Morale* in January, 1903. It appeared, then, after *Time and Free Will* and *Matter and Memory* and before *Creative Evolution;* and while containing ideas set forth in the first two of these works, it announces some of those which were afterwards developed in the last.

Though this book can in no sense be regarded as an epitome of the others, it yet forms the best introduction to them. M. Edouard Le Roy in his lately published book on M. Bergson's philosophy speaks of "this marvelously suggestive study which constitutes the best preface to the books themselves."

It has, however, more importance than a simple introduction would have, for in it M. Bergson explains, at greater length and in greater detail than in the other books, exactly what he means to convey by the word *intuition.* The intuitive method is treated independently and not, as elsewhere in his writings, incidentally, in its applications to particular problems. For this reason every writer who has attempted to give a complete exposition of M. Bergson's philosophy has been obliged to quote this essay at length; and it is indispensable therefore to the full understanding of its author's position. Translations into German, Italian, Hungarian, Polish, Swedish, and Russian have lately appeared, but the French original is at present out of print.

This translation has had the great advantage of being revised in proof by the author. I have to thank him for many alternative renderings, and also for a few slight alterations in the text, which he thought would make his meaning clearer.

T. E. HULME

St. John's College,
Cambridge

SELECTED BIBLIOGRAPHY

ENGLISH TRANSLATIONS OF BERGSON'S WORKS

Time and Free Will. New York, 1910.
Matter and Memory. New York, 1911.
Laughter. An Essay on the Meaning of the Comic. New York, 1911.
Introduction to Metaphysics. New York, 1913.
Creative Evolution. New York, 1911.
Mind-Energy. New York, 1920.
The Two Sources of Morality and Religion. London, 1935.
The Creative Mind. New York, 1946.

EXPOSITORY AND CRITICAL WORKS

Carr, H. Wildon, *Henri Bergson*. New York, 1912.
Chevalier, Jacques, *Henri Bergson*. New York, 1928.
Höffding, H., *Modern Philosophers (Lectures on Bergson)*. London, 1915.
Le Roy, E., *The New Philosophy of Henri Bergson*. New York, 1913.
Lindsay, A. D., *The Philosophy of Bergson*. London, 1911.
Maritain, Jacques, *La Philosophie Bergsonienne*. Paris, 1930.
Ruhe, A., *Henri Bergson*. London, 1914.
Scharfstein, Ben-Ami, *Roots of Bergson's Philosophy*. New York, 1943.
Solomon, J., *Bergson*. London, 1911.
Stephen, Karin, *The Misuse of Mind*. London, 1922.
Stewart, J. McK., *A Critical Exposition of Bergson's Philosophy*. London, 1912.

INTRODUCTION

I

WHEN HENRI BERGSON published *An Introduction to Metaphysics* as an essay in the *Revue de Métaphysique et de Morale* in 1903, he was already a distinguished figure in French thought. His reputation rested mainly on two works—the one known to the English-speaking world as *Time and Free Will* (1889), and *Matter and Memory* (1897). These books contained evidence of a strikingly original philosophy in the making, so that students awaited with interest its further elaboration. The appearance of *An Introduction to Metaphysics* did not disappoint them. Not only did it carry forward the development of Bergson's doctrine in important respects, but it also pointed the way towards the two major works that were to follow—*Creative Evolution* (1907) and *The Two Sources of Morality and Religion* (1932). Thus the essay which is here reproduced stands as a pivotal one in the thought of a leading philosopher of the twentieth century.

The outward details of Bergson's life reveal little that could be called dramatic. His career was almost entirely an adventure in the realm of mind. He was born in Paris on October 18, 1859, of an English mother and a Polish father. From the latter, who was an accomplished musician, he doubtless inherited something of the artistic temperament which is reflected throughout his books. In the course of the excellent education he received, his studies embraced the fields of literature, the natural sciences and philosophy. The scholastic record he left behind him was one of uniform brilliance. It was therefore not surprising that after obtaining the degree of *Agrégé* in 1881, he should have been appointed professor of philosophy at the Angers Lycée. A history of steady advancement by way of various other positions ensued; and the culminating point was reached in 1900 when he was elected to the chair of modern philosophy at the Collège de France—one of the highest academic posts in the nation. Here he remained until ill-health obliged him to retire in 1921. After the appearance of *Creative Evolution*, Bergson became a figure of international repute. People from all over the world came to Paris to hear him lecture, which he did with the same grace, felicity of phrase and originality of thought exhibited in his books. Yet neither the widespread adulation nor the many honors he received had any effect on his modest, unassuming personality. Like all genuinely great men he possessed true humility of soul. His death took place on January 5, 1941, amid the dark days which followed the Nazi occupation of France.

It is peculiarly appropriate that Bergson should have been born in the year which saw the publication of the *Origin of Species*.[1] For his philosophy can only be understood against the background provided by the theory of biological evolution. One of the central ideas put forward by Darwin was that the living beings who survived in the struggle for existence were able to do so because they had developed organs and ways of acting which adapted them to their environment. The presence of such characteristics was due to their efficacy in promoting survival. Now it was natural that this view should be extended to the mind as one of the functions possessed by living beings. Hence it was urged by some of Darwin's followers that the human intellect and the process of thinking are designed for wholly practical purposes. Their aim is to help the individual adjust himself to his world and to facilitate action.

This conception forms an essential part of Bergson's doctrine. The intellect is regarded by him as a kind of instrument or tool employed in the service of life. Just because of this, it has certain inherent limitations in its way of functioning. (1) The intellect apprehends the world externally as a collection of things in space. The very language we use to describe the world is saturated with spatial terms and metaphors.

---

[1] Two other "evolutionary" philosophers, John Dewey and Samuel Alexander, were also born in 1859.

(2) The intellect deals with the world by means of discrete units capable of being counted or measured. Consider the extent to which our daily lives are surrounded by numbers designating various kinds of units—dollars, miles, pounds, pages, etc. (3) The intellect treats the world as though it were fundamentally static and immobile. This is for Bergson the most serious limitation of all. For it means that the intellect is bound to misunderstand the fact of motion and change. Like a camera, it can only form a picture of a process by transforming the latter into a static image or series of images.

These limitations are clearly seen in the most typical product of the intellect—namely, the natural sciences. For the sciences seek always to state their results in mathematical terms. Thus, modern physics has been said to deal exclusively with pointer-readings and algebraic formulae. One result of this has been that phenomena like motion and time are analyzed into a succession of "points" and "instants." Indeed, even the time we are concerned with in everyday life is something determined by mechanical devices which designate purely spatial relations, like those indicated by the hands of a watch. Kant was right when he declared that we can only form a conception of time by drawing, either physically or in imagination, a geometrical line. What he failed to see, Bergson thinks, is the extent to which this "spatialization" of time falsifies it. In a similar manner, the sciences falsify the nature of motion by their mathematical representations of it. True, they cannot help doing so since they are expressions of the intellect, and have as their aim the practical control of the physical world. But for that very reason they need to be supplemented by intuition.

Such is the theme with which *An Introduction to Metaphysics* is mainly concerned. The discussion opens with a contrast between the two ways of knowing anything. The first is characteristic of the intellect which approaches the thing externally from some point of view alien to it, uses symbols to express its findings, and yields knowledge that is relative. The second is the process of intuition, whereby we "enter into" the thing and identify ourselves with it by a kind of "intellectual sympathy"—much as we identify ourselves with a figure in a novel we are reading. Here no symbols are involved, yet the knowledge attained is absolute and perfect. The former of these two ways of knowing is the method of the sciences. The latter is the proper method of metaphysics.

Bergson insists that we must not confuse intuition with mere feeling or emotion. Nor should we think of it as depending on some special faculty having a non-natural origin. Intuition is rather an act, or a series of acts, of direct participation in the immediacy of experience. It can be accomplished only by making an effort to detach oneself from the demands of action, by "inverting" the normal attitude of consciousness and immersing oneself in the current of direct awareness. The result will be a cognition of reality such as intellectual concepts can never yield. In so far as this reality is communicable, it must be expressed in metaphors or "fluid concepts" quite different from the static abstractions of logic. If metaphysics is to have any content at all it can only be through the use of the method thus delineated.

Now there is one object which is readily grasped by intuition—namely, our own personality. The existence which we know best is unquestionably our own. On this point Bergson agrees wholeheartedly with Descartes. Metaphysics must therefore begin by applying its method to the inner experience of the individual. What do we discover by so doing? According to Bergson, we discover the flowing of our personality through time. Or rather, since this way of speaking suggests the presence of an enduring self, what we ought to say is that we discover a ceaselessly changing process. The term which best conveys the character of the process is "duration" (*durée*) or pure time. Here we arrive at Bergson's most original conclusion. Absolute reality as revealed by metaphysical intuition is the ever-rolling stream of time.

In order to contrast duration with the mathematical, "spatialized" time of the intellect, Bergson offers certain additional descriptive comments. (1) Duration is a heterogeneous flux or becoming. (2) It is irreversible, straining always towards the future. (3) It is continually creating newness or novelty, and hence is intrinsically unpredictable. (4) It is the inexhaustible source of freedom. (5) Its living reality can never be communicated by images or concepts, but must be directly intuited. "If a man is incapable of getting for himself the intuition of the constitutive duration of his own being," Bergson insists, "nothing will ever give it to him, concepts no more than images." Time will only confess its secrets to him who practices the art of "intellectual auscultation."

Once we have grasped the inner nature of becoming, it is possible for us to understand that form of it which appears as movement in space. Consider the insoluble paradoxes which arise when the intellect endeavors to explain motion in terms of "points" and "instants." An illustration from the ancient philosopher, Zeno of Elea, will disclose the difficulty. Take the phenomenon of a flying arrow. It is easy to show, says Zeno, that it does not really move. For at each instant of its flight it occupies one and only one point of space. This means that at each instant the arrow must be at rest, since otherwise it would not occupy a given point at that instant. But its whole course is composed of such points. Therefore, the arrow does not actually move at all. Bergson agrees that the argument as stated is irrefutable. What he denies is Zeno's assumption that the arrow can literally *be* at a point. The most we can say is that it "passes through" a point. But strictly speaking, the points in its trajectory are not real positions. They are "suppositions" of the intellect. Thus the moral to be drawn from Zeno's paradoxes is not that motion is impossible, but rather that it is impossible for the intellect to comprehend motion. Just as duration can never be "constructed" in terms of instants, so movement can never be "constructed" in terms of points. Both time and motion have to be apprehended intuitively.

It follows from the above that philosophies which employ the method of rational thought are foredoomed to failure. For they are attempting to gain disinterested knowledge of the real by a process whose aim is practical. No wonder their efforts have ended either in unwarranted dogmatism or in futile skepticism! Rationalism and empiricism are equally at fault here. The former seeks to interpret the world in the light of some fixed structure of thought, and so produces such notions as the Forms of Plato or the Categories of Kant. Traditional empiricism, on the other hand, while it turns to experience, regards the latter as composed of static "elements" like the Impressions of Hume or the Sensations of J. S. Mill. Both schools thus assume that the changing must be explained by the permanent, that there is more in the immutable than in the moving, and that we pass from the stable to the unstable by mere diminution. Neither group take becoming seriously. This is for Bergson the cardinal error of classical philosophy. It can only be corrected by a true empiricism which tries to apprehend experience in its living reality as a continuous, changing process. "And this true empiricism is the true metaphysics."

The question arises as to the connection between the relative knowledge of the sciences and the absolute knowledge reached by metaphysical intuition. A critical reader will not fail to observe a certain wavering in the essay on this point. Sometimes Bergson appears to be saying that the contributions of the intellect and of intuition simply supplement one another. For example, he admits that modern mathematics has created in the infinitesimal calculus a method of grasping motion "no longer from without and in its displayed result, but from within and in its tendency to change." Yet the calculus is obliged to use symbols, and hence to introduce a degree of immutability into its interpretations. For this reason it needs to be supplemented by the non-symbolic intuition of metaphysics which presents the concrete fact of motion. When thinking thus, Bergson denies that he is "anti-intellectual" or "anti-scientific." [2] Metaphysics, he insists, does not oppose the sciences. It complements them.

[2] See his vigorous statements on this point quoted in Ruhe, *Henri Bergson*, pp. 37-40.

At other times, however, Bergson adopts a different view. Metaphysics establishes the conclusion that reality is mobility. If so, what the intellect gives us must be mere appearance. For the intellect traffics in stable perceptions and static conceptions; and neither of these yield an accurate picture of the world. It surely follows that the results of the sciences are not *knowledge* in any proper sense of the term. These results are practically efficacious, but not *true*. Indeed, they falsify the actual character of the world in the interests of action. The terminal point of this line of thought can only be a type of mysticism. Reality is known intuitively, not discursively. The concepts of the intellect are unable to communicate it. Such was the direction in which Bergson's thought was moving as he completed *An Introduction to Metaphysics*.

II

The final pages of the essay discuss several propositions which express the broader implications of Bergson's philosophy. What is said can scarcely be understood without some knowledge of the position elaborated in his later works. It may therefore serve a useful purpose if we add a summary statement of that position, with special reference to *Creative Evolution*.

This remarkable book is a philosophical interpretation of biology which culminates in a sweeping metaphysical vision, not unlike that of Plotinus. The path leading to the vision is cleared by examining and rejecting four major conceptions of evolution—the Darwinian, the neo-Lamarckian, the Spencerian, and DeVries' theory of mutations. In place of these Bergson offers his own original view of what evolution ought to mean for the philosopher.

Both Darwin and DeVries stress the idea of accidental variations among members of a species competing with one another in the struggle for existence. Variations which are favorable enable their possessors to survive, whereas unfavorable variations lead to extinction. Darwin thought all such changes were minute and gradual. DeVries held that they were sudden. Bergson argues that neither doctrine offers a satisfactory account of evolution. Both overlook the functional unity which is essential to every organism, a unity which would require that any variation in one part be accompanied by automatic variations in all other parts, so that the organism could continue its activity. But by what mysterious agency is this coordination effected? Darwin and DeVries have no answer. Their theory fails to explain how continuity of function can be maintained through successive alterations of form.

The neo-Lamarckian theory escapes this particular objection by regarding variations as due to the use which a living being makes of its capacities. Certain organisms put forth greater "effort" in the struggle for existence than others. In so doing, they develop characteristics favorable to survival, while their less energetic brethren fall by the wayside. Yet the validity of this approach depends on the transmission of the acquired characteristics from one generation to the next; and the positive evidence for such transmission is highly inconclusive. Moreover, Bergson insists, we can hardly suppose that the mechanism of evolution is to be found in the "effort" expended by individual organisms, for this would base the whole developmental process on something sporadic and contingent. If the notion of "effort" is to be introduced, it must be understood in a far deeper sense than that of the neo-Lamarckians.

Finally, there is the evolutionary philosophy of Spencer. It, too, rests on the dubious assumption of the transmission of acquired characteristics (e.g., habits). But what is far worse, this philosophy turns out on examination not to be a genuine evolutionism at all. It is rather a mechanistic attempt to reduce development to the integration of matter and the dissipation of motion. Real becoming is given no recognition by Spencer. His position is just a thinly disguised materialism, which tries to reconstruct evolution out of a number of unchanging elements.

None of these theories succeed in answering the question why evolution has so far followed the course which it has in fact taken. If the only consideration involved is success in maintaining life, why did the process not stop with those elementary organisms that are as well, or better, adapted than human beings to the conditions of existence? Why has life gone on complicating itself more and more dangerously? Because, Bergson contends, a vital impulse *(élan vital)* is driving it towards ever higher levels of organization. This impulse constitutes the unique nature of all that is animate. It is the fundamental cause of the variations which produce new species. And as the ultimate principle of existence, it is the creative power which rolls through all things.

Can the intellect form an adequate conception of the *élan vital?* It would seem not. Just as in the case of time and motion, the intellect deals with life by translating it into static and mechanical terms. Here again it falsifies in the interests of practice. To grasp the nature of life, therefore, we must turn to intuition. In pure duration we get a feeling of our own evolution and of the evolution of the cosmos. Such a feeling may then be communicated, at least partly, in analogies and metaphors; and these Bergson is supremely adept at providing. Thus he compares the vital impulse to a jet of steam spurting into the air continually, condensing into myriads of drops, and falling back to the source. The drops represent the purely material aspect of the universe against which life wages ceaseless battle. At the summit of the jet, where a small part of the steam remains uncondensed for some seconds, we have the analogue of the living species thrown up by evolution. The original impulsion sustains the individual members of the species, until each after his brief career passes away into dead matter. But even this image, Bergson warns us, is a feeble representation of reality. For the jet of steam and the forming of drops of water are determined necessarily by physical laws, whereas the perpetual creation of the world is a free act, and life within the material world participates in that freedom.

One distinctive feature of the above view is its rejection of any final goal for the evolutionary process. There is no far-off divine event towards which the whole creation moves. Bergson will have nothing to do with this kind of external teleology or "radical finalism." He regards it as another attempt to make time a subordinate aspect of the cosmos, since if things are merely realizing a program previously arranged, no creativity and therefore no genuine change are occurring. In that case, "time is useless." Hence radical finalism is only inverted mechanism, as can be seen in the thought of an extreme teleologist like Leibniz. For Bergson there can be no "pre-established harmony." On the contrary, harmony is ever in the making, and ever emerging in novel forms. The course of evolution is intrinsically unpredictable.

Another facet of Bergson's theory is that cosmic development is not construed as a linear process. The vital impulse expresses itself in a multitude of divergent tendencies. Even the history of living forms on the earth reveals three distinct evolutionary lines. One of these led to the vegetable kingdom where supine security reigns supreme. The second gave rise to the arthropods, whose mobility is subject to the iron rule of instinct, such as obtains among bees and ants. The third line produced the vertebrates and eventually man. Here the emergence of intellect made possible the achievement of freedom. For intellect became a powerful means of gaining control over matter, and thus released man to some degree from the pressure of material needs. He was then in a position to cultivate the fragile and flickering power of intuition through which ultimate reality is revealed to him. It is in this quite special sense that man may be considered the "end" of evolution.

The precise status of matter in Bergson's metaphysics is a difficult question. Ostensibly, it is the form the *élan vital* assumes when, in the course of its outpouring, the primal energy begins to be dissipated. Matter is a sort of "devitalized" life, and hence exhibits a steady degradation of energy as described by the Second Law of Thermodynamics. There is still a ceaseless movement, but in a direction "opposite to" that of life.

One function of the intellect is to present the continuous flux of matter in the guise of static, discrete objects. Thus, when we perceive a sensory quality like yellow, our visual apparatus is condensing trillions of vibrations into one stable appearance. Our minds immediately interpret this as a yellow surface located in a certain region of space. But the reality itself has no such simple location.[3] Vibrations stream out indefinitely and interpenetrate with all the other vibrations in the physical world. From the flux of energy, the intellect "carves" individual things and happenings. Presumably, then, if we mean by "matter" the ordinary furniture of earth— stones, clouds, tables, etc.—the word designates nothing real. Its use must be restricted to the dynamic processes which are investigated by physics. Hence, as Bergson puts it, "matter is weighted with geometry." To what extent this reduces the idea to a fiction from the standpoint of metaphysics remains obscure.

Is the vital impulse to be thought of as a conscious or psychical activity? In *Creative Evolution* Bergson tends to be cautious when faced with that question, though he does speak at one point of "the consciousness, or rather supra-consciousness, that is at the origin of life." He even suggests the possibility of applying the term "God" to the source from which all things flow. These tentative remarks, however, receive no elaboration; and it was not until the publication of his last work, *The Two Sources of Morality and Religion*, that their full meaning began to appear. In this book, the primal energy at the heart of the universe is affirmed to be love. Hence the most appropriate word to symbolize it is "God." Bergson accepts the view of the Christian mystics that "God is love and the object of love." This truth is certified by intuition when it rises to the heights of mystical experience, where union with the Divine is achieved. The content of such experience must be forever ineffable. But to the philosopher who has thus apprehended the *élan vital*, creation will appear "as God

[3] Whitehead was later to make the same point in his *Science and the Modern World*, Ch. V; but the idea goes back at least to Faraday.

undertaking to create creators, that he may have, besides himself, beings worthy of his love."

Despite the felicitous language in which it is expressed and the wealth of empirical detail it surveys, the Bergsonian metaphysics contains many mysteries. Few students, for example, will discover a clear account of the relation between *durée* and the vital impulse, or between matter and life. Some may be puzzled by the paradox of a philosophy which discredits the intellect on the grounds of a theory (biological evolution) which is itself the product of the intellect. And so on. Perhaps these difficulties are unavoidable in the work of a mind at bottom mystical and unsympathetic to logic. "He is persuasive without argument," Santayana once remarked; and the observation is in the main a just one. Those who believe that philosophy must employ the intellect in the search for truth may be fascinated by Bergson's eloquence, but they will hardly be convinced.

Nevertheless, his books have won a permanent place in the history of recent thought. Nowhere else do we find so vivid a portrayal of the temporal dimension of existence, or so impressive an account of the uniqueness of life. Bergson stimulates us anew to think on these things. By directing our attention to immediate experience, he enables us to see the novelty ingredient in each fresh moment—a novelty mechanistic theories seek to deny. At the very center of the actual he discerns the freedom and creativity which are conditions of the next development in man. It is as a reporter of such matters that Bergson displays his greatest gifts. The reader will meet many illustrations of this in the brilliant pages which follow.

THOMAS A. GOUDGE

UNIVERSITY OF TORONTO
February, 1949

An Introduction to Metaphysics

A COMPARISON of the definitions of metaphysics and the various concepts of the absolute leads to the discovery that philosophers, in spite of their apparent divergencies, agree in distinguishing two profoundly different ways of knowing a thing. The first implies that we move round the object; the second, that we enter into it. The first depends on the point of view at which we are placed and on the symbols by which we express ourselves. The second neither depends on a point of view nor relies on any symbol. The first kind of knowledge may be said to stop at the *relative;* the second, in those cases where it is possible, to attain the *absolute.*

Consider, for example, the movement of an object in space. My perception of the motion will vary with the point of view, moving or stationary, from which I observe it. My expression of it will vary with the systems of axes, or the points of reference, to which I relate it; that is, with the symbols by which I translate it. For this double reason I call such motion *relative:* in the one case, as in the other, I am placed outside the object itself. But when I speak of an *absolute* movement, I am attributing to the moving object an interior and, so to speak, states of mind; I also imply that I am in sympathy with those states, and that I insert myself in them by an effort of imagination. Then, according as the object is moving or stationary, according as it adopts one movement or another, what I experience will vary. And what I experience will depend neither on the point of view I may take up in regard to the object, since I am inside the object itself, nor on the symbols by which I may translate the motion, since I have rejected all translations in order to possess the original. In short, I shall no longer grasp the movement from without, remaining where

I am, but from where it is, from within, as it is in itself. I shall possess an absolute.

Consider, again, a character whose adventures are related to me in a novel. The author may multiply the traits of his hero's character, may make him speak and act as much as he pleases, but all this can never be equivalent to the simple and indivisible feeling which I should experience if I were able for an instant to identify myself with the person of the hero himself. Out of that indivisible feeling, as from a spring, all the words, gestures, and actions of the man would appear to me to flow naturally. They would no longer be accidents which, added to the idea I had already formed of the character, continually enriched that idea, without ever completing it. The character would be given to me all at once, in its entirety, and the thousand incidents which manifest it, instead of adding themselves to the idea and so enriching it, would seem to me, on the contrary, to detach themselves from it, without, however, exhausting it or impoverishing its essence. All the things I am told about the man provide me with so many points of view from which I can observe him. All the traits which describe him, and which can make him known to me only by so many comparisons with persons or things I know already, are signs by which he is expressed more or less symbolically. Symbols and points of view, therefore, place me outside him; they give me only what he has in common with others, and not what belongs to him and to him alone. But that which is properly himself, that which constitutes his essence, cannot be perceived from without, being internal by definition, nor be expressed by symbols, being incommensurable with everything else. Description, history, and analysis leave me here in the relative. Coincidence with the person himself would alone give me the absolute.

It is in this sense, and in this sense only, that *absolute* is synonymous with *perfection*. Were all the photographs of a town, taken from all possible points of view, to go on indefinitely completing one another, they would never be equivalent to the solid town in which we walk about. Were all the translations of a poem into all possible languages to add together their various shades of meaning and, correcting each other by a kind of mutual retouching, to give a more and more faithful image of the poem they translate, they would yet never succeed in rendering the inner meaning of the original. A representation taken from a certain point of view, a translation made with certain symbols, will always remain imperfect in comparison with the object of which a view has been taken, or which the symbols seek to express. But the absolute, which is the object and not its representation, the original and not its translation, is perfect, by being perfectly what it is.

It is doubtless for this reason that the *absolute* has often been identified with the *infinite*. Suppose that I wished to communicate to someone who did not know Greek the extraordinarily simple impression that a passage in Homer makes upon me; I should first give a translation of the lines, I should then comment on my translation, and then develop the commentary; in this way, by piling up explanation on explanation, I might approach nearer and nearer to what I wanted to express; but I should never quite reach it. When you raise your arm, you accomplish a movement of which you have, from within, a simple perception; but for me, watching it from the outside, your arm passes through one point, then through another, and between these two there will be still other points; so that, if I began to count, the operation would go on forever. Viewed from the inside, then, an absolute is a simple thing; but looked at from the outside, that is to say, relatively to other things, it becomes, in relation to these signs which express it, the gold coin for which we never seem able to finish giving small change. Now, that which lends itself at the same time both to an indivisible apprehension and to an inexhaustible enumeration is, by the very definition of the word, an infinite.

It follows from this that an absolute could only be given in an *intuition*, whilst everything else falls within the province of *analysis*. By intuition is meant the kind of *intellectual sympathy* by which one places oneself within an object in order to coincide with what is unique in it and consequently inexpressible. Analysis, on the contrary, is the operation which reduces the object to elements already known, that is, to elements common both to it and other objects. To analyze, therefore, is to express a thing as a function of something other than itself. All analysis is thus a translation, a development into symbols, a representation taken from successive points of view from which we note as many resemblances as possible between the new object which we are studying and others which we believe we know already. In its eternally unsatisfied desire to embrace the object around which it is compelled to turn, analysis multiplies without end the number of its points of view in order to complete its always incomplete representation, and ceaselessly varies its symbols that it may perfect the always imperfect translation. It goes on, therefore, to infinity. But intuition, if intuition is possible, is a simple act.

Now it is easy to see that the ordinary function of positive science is analysis. Positive science works, then, above all, with symbols. Even the most concrete of the natural sciences, those concerned with life, confine themselves to the visible form of living beings, their organs and anatomical elements. They make comparisons between these forms, they reduce the more complex to the more simple; in short, they study the workings of life in what is, so to speak, only its visual symbol. If there exists any means of possessing a reality absolutely instead of knowing it relatively, of placing oneself within it instead of looking at it from outside points of view, of having the intuition instead of making the analysis: in short, of seizing it without any expression, translation, or symbolic representation—metaphysics is that means. *Metaphysics, then, is the science which claims to dispense with symbols.*

*

*   *

There is one reality, at least, which we all seize from within, by intuition and not by simple analysis. It is our own personality in its flowing through time—our self which endures. We may sympathize intellectually with nothing else, but we certainly sympathize with our own selves.

When I direct my attention inward to contemplate my own self (supposed for the moment to be inactive), I perceive at first, as a crust solidified on the surface, all the perceptions which come to it from the material world. These perceptions are clear, distinct, juxtaposed or juxtaposable one with another; they tend to group themselves into objects. Next, I notice the memories which more or less adhere to these perceptions and which serve to interpret them. These memories have been detached, as it were, from the depth of my personality, drawn to the surface by the perceptions which resemble them; they rest on the surface of my mind without being absolutely myself. Lastly, I feel the stir of tendencies and motor habits—a crowd of virtual actions, more or less firmly bound to these perceptions and memories. All these clearly defined elements appear more distinct from me, the more distinct they are from each other. Radiating, as they do, from within outwards, they form, collectively, the surface of a sphere which tends to grow larger and lose itself in the exterior world. But if I draw myself in from the periphery towards the center, if I search in the depth of my being that which is most uniformly, most constantly, and most enduringly myself, I find an altogether different thing.

There is, beneath these sharply cut crystals and this frozen surface, a continuous flux which is not comparable to any flux I have ever seen. There is a succession of states, each of which announces that which follows and contains that which precedes it. They can, properly speaking, only be said to form multiple states when I have already passed them and turn back to observe their track. Whilst I was experiencing them they were so solidly organized, so profoundly animated with a common life, that I could not have said where any one of them finished or where another commenced. In reality no one of them begins or ends, but all extend into each other.

This inner life may be compared to the unrolling of a coil, for there is no living being who does not feel himself coming gradually to the end of his role; and to live is to grow old. But it may just as well be compared to a continual rolling up, like that of a thread on a ball, for our past follows us, it swells incessantly with the present that it picks up on its way; and consciousness means memory.

But actually it is neither an unrolling nor a rolling up, for these two similes evoke the idea of lines and surfaces whose parts are homogeneous and superposable on one another. Now, there are no two identical moments in the life of the same conscious being. Take the simplest sensation, suppose it constant, absorb in it the entire personality: the conscious-ness which will accompany this sensation cannot remain iden-tical with itself for two consecutive moments, because the second moment always contains, over and above the first, the memory that the first has bequeathed to it. A consciousness which could experience two identical moments would be a consciousness without memory. It would die and be born again continually. In what other way could one represent unconsciousness?

It would be better, then, to use as a comparison the myriad-tinted spectrum, with its insensible gradations leading from one shade to another. A current of feeling which passed along the spectrum, assuming in turn the tint of each of its shades, would experience a series of gradual changes, each of which would announce the one to follow and would sum up those which preceded it. Yet even here the successive shades of the spectrum always remain external one to another. They are juxtaposed; they occupy space. But pure duration, on the contrary, excludes all idea of juxtaposition, reciprocal exter-nality, and extension.

Let us, then, rather, imagine an infinitely small elastic body, contracted, if it were possible, to a mathematical point. Let this be drawn out gradually in such a manner that from the point comes a constantly lengthening line. Let us fix our attention not on the line as a line, but on the action by which it is traced. Let us bear in mind that this action, in spite of its duration, is indivisible if accomplished without stopping, that if a stopping-point is inserted, we have two actions instead of one, that each of these separate actions is then the indivisible operation of which we speak, and that it is not the moving action itself which is divisible, but, rather, the stationary line it leaves behind it as its track in space. Finally, let us free ourselves from the space which underlies the movement in order to consider only the movement itself, the act of tension or extension; in short, pure mobility. We shall have this time a more faithful image of the development of our self in duration.

However, even this image is incomplete, and, indeed, every comparison will be insufficient, because the unrolling of our duration resembles in some of its aspects the unity of an advancing movement and in others the multiplicity of expanding states; and, clearly, no metaphor can express one of these two aspects without sacrificing the other. If I use the comparison of the spectrum with its thousand shades, I have before me a thing already made, whilst duration is continually in the making. If I think of an elastic which is being stretched, or of a spring which is extended or relaxed, I forget the richness of color, characteristic of duration that is lived, to see only the simple movement by which consciousness passes from one shade to another. The inner life is all this at once: variety of qualities, continuity of progress, and unity of direction. It cannot be represented by images.

But it is even less possible to represent it by *concepts,* that is by abstract, general, or simple ideas. It is true that no image can reproduce exactly the original feeling I have of the flow of my own conscious life. But it is not even necessary that I should attempt to render it. If a man is incapable of getting for himself the intuition of the constitutive duration of his own being, nothing will ever give it to him, concepts no more than images. Here the single aim of the philosopher should be to promote a certain effort, which in most men is usually fettered by habits of mind more useful to life. Now the image has at least this advantage, that it keeps us in the concrete. No image can replace the intuition of duration, but many diverse images, borrowed from very different orders of things, may, by the convergence of their action, direct consciousness to the precise point where there is a certain intuition to be seized. By choosing images as dissimilar as possible, we shall prevent any one of them from usurping the place of the intuition it is intended to call up, since it would then be driven away at once by its rivals. By providing that, in spite of their differences of aspect, they all require from the mind the same kind of attention, and in some sort the same degree of tension, we shall gradually accustom consciousness to a particular and clearly-defined disposition—that precisely which it must adopt in order to appear to itself as it really is, without any veil. But, then, consciousness must at least consent to make the effort. For it will have been shown nothing: It will simply have been placed in the attitude it must take up in order to make the desired effort, and so come by itself to the intuition. Concepts, on the contrary—especially if they are simple—have the disadvantage of being in reality symbols substituted for the object they symbolize, and demand no effort on our part. Examined closely, each of them, it would be seen, retains only that part of the object which is common to it and to others, and expresses, still more than the image does, a *comparison* between the object and others which resemble it. But as the comparison has made manifest a resemblance, as the resemblance is a property of the object, and as a property has every appearance of being a *part* of the object which possesses it, we easily persuade ourselves that by setting concept beside concept we are reconstructing the whole of the object with its parts, thus obtaining, so to speak, its intellectual equivalent. In this way we believe that we can form a faithful representation of duration by setting in line the concepts of unity, multiplicity, continuity, finite or infinite divisibility, etc. There precisely is the illusion. There also is the danger. Just in so far as abstract ideas can render service to analysis, that is, to the scientific study of the object in its relations to other objects, so far are they incapable of replacing intuition, that is, the metaphysical investigation of what is essential and unique in the object. For, on the one hand, these concepts, laid side by side, never actually give us more than an artificial reconstruction of the object, of which they can only symbolize certain general and, in a way, impersonal aspects; it is therefore useless to believe that with them we can seize a reality of which they present to us the shadow alone. And, on the other hand, besides the illusion there is also a very serious danger. For the concept generalizes at the same time as it abstracts. The concept can only symbolize a particular property by making it common to an infinity of things. It therefore always more or less deforms the property by the extension it gives to it. Replaced in the metaphysical object to which it belongs, a property coincides with the object, or at least molds itself on it, and adopts the same outline. Extracted from the metaphysical object, and presented in a concept, it grows indefinitely larger, and goes beyond the object itself, since henceforth it has to contain it, along with a number of other objects. Thus the different concepts that we form of the properties of a thing inscribe round it so many circles, each much too large and none of them fitting it exactly. And yet, in the thing itself the properties coincided with the thing, and coincided consequently with one another. So that if we are bent on reconstructing the object with concepts, some artifice must be sought whereby this coincidence of the object and its properties can be brought about. For example, we may choose one of the concepts and try, starting from it, to get round to the others. But we shall then soon discover that according as we start from one concept or another, the meeting and combination of the concepts will take place in an altogether different way. According as we start, for example, from unity or from multiplicity, we shall have to conceive differently the multiple unity of duration. Everything will depend on the weight we attribute to this or that concept, and this weight will always be arbitrary, since the concept extracted from the object has no weight, being only the shadow of a body. In this way, as many different *systems* will spring up as there are external points of view from which the reality can be examined, or larger circles in which it can be enclosed. Simple concepts have, then, not only the inconvenience of dividing the concrete unity of the object into so many symbolical expressions; they also divide philosophy into distinct schools, each of which takes its seat, chooses its counters, and carries on with the others a game that will never end. Either metaphysics is only this play of ideas, or else, if it is a serious occupation of the mind, if it is a science and not simply an exercise, it must transcend concepts in order to reach intuition. Certainly, concepts are necessary to it, for all the other sciences work as a rule with concepts, and metaphysics cannot dispense with the other sciences. But it is only truly itself when it goes beyond the concept, or at least when it frees itself from rigid and ready-made concepts in order to create a kind very different from those which we habitually use; I mean supple, mobile, and almost fluid representations, always ready to mold themselves on the fleeting forms of intuition. We shall return later to this important point. Let it suffice us for the moment to have shown that our duration can be presented to us directly in an intuition, that it can be suggested to us indirectly by images, but that it can never—if we confine the word concept to its proper meaning —be enclosed in a conceptual representation.

Let us try for an instant to consider our duration as a multiplicity. It will then be necessary to add that the terms of this multiplicity, instead of being distinct, as they are in any other multiplicity, encroach on one another; and that while we can no doubt, by an effort of imagination, solidify duration once it has elapsed, divide it into juxtaposed portions and count all these portions, yet this operation is accomplished on the frozen memory of the duration, on the stationary trace which the mobility of duration leaves behind it, and not on the duration itself. We must admit, therefore, that if there is a multiplicity here, it bears no resemblance to any other multiplicity we know. Shall we say, then, that duration has unity? Doubtless, a continuity of elements which prolong themselves into one another participates in unity as much as in multiplicity; but this moving, changing, colored, living unity has hardly anything in common with the abstract, motionless, and empty unity which the concept of pure unity circumscribes. Shall we conclude from this that duration must be defined as unity and multiplicity at the same time? But singularly enough, however much I manipulate the two concepts, portion them out, combine them differently, practice on them the most subtle operations of mental chemistry, I never obtain anything which resembles the simple intuition that I have of duration; while, on the contrary, when I replace myself in duration by an effort of intuition, I immediately perceive how it is unity, multiplicity, and many other things besides. These different concepts, then, were only so many standpoints from which we could consider duration. Neither separated nor reunited have they made us penetrate into it.

We do penetrate into it, however, and that can only be by an effort of intuition. In this sense, an inner, absolute knowledge of the duration of the self by the self is possible. But if metaphysics here demands and can obtain an intuition, science has none the less need of an analysis. Now it is a confusion between the function of analysis and that of intuition which gives birth to the discussions between the schools and the conflicts between systems.

Psychology, in fact, proceeds like all the other sciences by analysis. It resolves the self, which has been given to it at first in a simple intuition, into sensations, feelings, ideas, etc., which it studies separately. It substitutes, then, for the self a series of elements which form the facts of psychology. But are these *elements* really *parts?* That is the whole question, and it is because it has been evaded that the problem of human personality has so often been stated in insoluble terms.

It is incontestable that every psychical state, simply because it belongs to a person, reflects the whole of a personality. Every feeling, however simple it may be, contains virtually within it the whole past and present of the being experiencing it, and, consequently, can only be separated and constituted into a "state" by an effort of abstraction or of analysis. But it is no less incontestable that without this effort of abstraction or analysis there would be no possible development of the science of psychology. What, then, exactly, is the operation by which a psychologist detaches a mental state in order to erect it into a more or less independent entity? He begins by neglecting that special coloring of the personality which cannot be expressed in known and common terms. Then he endeavors to isolate, in the person already thus simplified, some aspect which lends itself to an interesting inquiry. If he is considering inclination, for example, he will neglect the inexpressible shade which colors it, and which makes the inclination mine and not yours; he will fix his attention on the movement by which our personality *leans toward* a certain object: he will isolate this attitude, and it is this special aspect of the personality, this snapshot of the mobility of the inner life, this "diagram" of concrete inclination, that he will erect into an independent fact. There is in this something very like what an artist passing through Paris does when he makes, for example, a sketch of a tower of Notre Dame. The tower is inseparably united to the building, which is itself no less inseparably united to the ground, to its surroundings, to the whole of Paris, and so on. It is first necessary to detach it from all these; only one aspect of the whole is noted, that formed by the tower of Notre Dame. Moreover, the special form of this tower is due to the grouping of the stones of which it is composed; but the artist does not concern himself with these stones, he notes only the silhouette of the tower. For the real and internal organization of the thing he substitutes, then, an external and schematic representation. So that, on the whole, his sketch corresponds to an observation of the object from a certain point of view and to the choice of a certain means of representation. But exactly the same thing holds true of the operation by which the psychologist extracts a single mental state from the whole personality. This isolated psychical state is hardly anything but a sketch, the commencement of an artificial reconstruction; it is the whole considered under a certain elementary aspect in which we are specially interested and which we have carefully noted. It is not a part, but an element. It has not been obtained by a natural dismemberment, but by analysis.

Now beneath all the sketches he has made at Paris the visitor will probably, by way of memento, write the word "Paris." And as he has really seen Paris, he will be able, with the help of the original intuition he had of the whole, to place his sketches therein, and so join them up together. But there is no way of performing the inverse operation; it is impossible, even with an infinite number of accurate sketches, and even with the word "Paris" which indicates that they must be combined together, to get back to an intuition that one has never had, and to give oneself an impression of what Paris is like if one has never seen it. This is because we are not dealing here with real *parts*, but with mere *notes* of the total impression. To take a still more striking example, where the notation is more completely symbolic, suppose that I am shown, mixed together at random, the letters which make up a poem I am ignorant of. If the letters were *parts* of the poem, I could attempt to reconstitute the poem with them by trying the different possible arrangements, as a child does with the pieces of a Chinese puzzle. But I should never for a moment think of attempting such a thing in this case, because the letters are not *component parts*, but only *partial expressions*, which is quite a different thing. That is why, if I know the poem, I at once put each of the letters in its proper place and join them up without difficulty by a continuous connection, whilst the inverse operation is impossible. Even when I believe I am actually attempting this inverse operation, even when I put the letters end to end, I begin by thinking of some plausible meaning. I thereby give myself an intuition, and from this intuition I attempt to redescend to the elementary symbols which would reconstitute its expression. The very idea of reconstituting a thing by operations practiced on symbolic elements alone implies such an absurdity that it would never occur to anyone if they recollected that they were not dealing with fragments of the thing, but only, as it were, with fragments of its symbol.

Such is, however, the undertaking of the philosophers who try to reconstruct personality with psychical states, whether they confine themselves to those states alone, or whether they add a kind of thread for the purpose of joining the states together. Both empiricists and rationalists are victims of the same fallacy. Both of them mistake *partial notations* for *real parts,* thus confusing the point of view of analysis and of intuition, of science and of metaphysics.

The empiricists say quite rightly that psychological analysis discovers nothing more in personality than psychical states. Such is, in fact, the function, and the very definition of analysis. The psychologist has nothing else to do but analyze personality, that is, to note certain states; at the most he may put the label "ego" on these states in saying they are "states of the ego," just as the artist writes the word "Paris" on each of his sketches. On the level at which the psychologist places himself, and on which he must place himself, the "ego" is only a sign by which the primitive, and moreover very confused, intuition which has furnished the psychologist with his subject-matter is recalled; it is only a word, and the great error here lies in believing that while remaining on the same level we can find behind the word a thing. Such has been the error of those philosophers who have not been able to resign themselves to being only psychologists in psychology, Taine and Stuart Mill, for example. Psychologists in the method they apply, they have remained metaphysicians in the object they set before themselves. They desire an intuition, and by a strange inconsistency they seek this intuition in analysis which is the very negation of it. They look for the ego, and they claim to find it in psychical states, though this diversity of states has itself only been obtained, and could only be obtained, by transporting oneself outside the ego altogether, so as to make a series of sketches, notes, and more or less symbolic and schematic diagrams. Thus, however much they place the states side by side, multiplying points of contact and exploring the intervals, the ego always escapes them, so that they finish by seeing in it nothing but a vain phantom. We might as well deny that the *Iliad* had a meaning, on the ground that we had looked in vain for that meaning in the intervals between the letters of which it is composed.

Philosophical empiricism is born here, then, of a confusion between the point of view of intuition and that of analysis. Seeking for the original in the translation, where naturally it cannot be, it denies the existence of the original on the ground that it is not found in the translation. It leads of necessity to negations; but on examining the matter closely, we perceive that these negations simply mean that analysis is not intuition, which is self-evident. From the original, and, one must add, very indistinct intuition which gives positive science its material, science passes immediately to analysis, which multiplies to infinity its observations of this material from outside points of view. It soon comes to believe that by putting together all these diagrams it can reconstitute the object itself. No wonder, then, that it sees this object fly before it, like a child that would like to make a solid plaything out of the shadows outlined along the wall!

But rationalism is the dupe of the same illusion. It starts out from the same confusion as empiricism, and remains equally powerless to reach the inner self. Like empiricism, it considers psychical states as so many fragments detached from an ego that binds them together. Like empiricism, it tries to join these fragments together in order to re-create the unity of the self. Like empiricism, finally, it sees this unity of the self, in the continually renewed effort it makes to clasp it, steal away indefinitely like a phantom. But whilst empiricism, weary of the struggle, ends by declaring that there is nothing else but the multiplicity of psychical states, rationalism persists in affirming the unity of the person. It is true that, seeking this unity on the level of the psychical states themselves, and obliged, besides, to put down to the account of these states all the qualities and determinations that it finds by analysis (since analysis by its very definition leads always to *states*), nothing is left to it, for the unity of personality, but something purely negative, the absence of all determination. The psychical states having

necessarily in this analysis taken and kept for themselves everything that can serve as matter, the "unity of the ego" can never
be more than a form without content. It will be absolutely
indeterminate and absolutely void. To these detached psychical states, to these shadows of the ego, the sum of which was
for the empiricists the equivalent of the self, rationalism, in
order to reconstitute personality, adds something still more
unreal, the void in which these shadows move—a place for
shadows, one might say. How could this "form," which is in
truth formless, serve to characterize a living, active, concrete
personality, or to distinguish Peter from Paul? Is it astonishing that the philosophers who have isolated this "form" of
personality should, then, find it insufficient to characterize a
definite person, and that they should be gradually led to make
their empty ego a kind of bottomless receptacle, which belongs
no more to Peter than to Paul, and in which there is room,
according to our preference, for entire humanity, for God, or
for existence in general? I see in this matter only one difference between empiricism and rationalism. The former, seeking
the unity of the ego in the gaps, as it were, between the psychical states, is led to fill the gaps with other states, and so on
indefinitely, so that the ego, compressed in a constantly nar-
rowing interval, tends towards zero, as analysis is pushed farther and farther; whilst rationalism, making the ego the place
where mental states are lodged, is confronted with an empty
space which we have no reason to limit here rather than there,
which goes beyond each of the successive boundaries that we
try to assign to it, which constantly grows larger, and which
tends to lose itself no longer in zero, but in the infinite.

The distance, then, between a so-called "empiricism" like
that of Taine and the most transcendental speculations of certain German pantheists is very much less than is generally supposed. The method is analogous in both cases; it consists in
reasoning about the *elements* of a translation as if they were
parts of the original. But a true empiricism is that which
proposes to get as near to the original itself as possible, to
search deeply into its life, and so, by a kind of *intellectual*

auscultation, to feel the throbbings of its soul; and this true empiricism is the true metaphysics. It is true that the task is an extremely difficult one, for none of the ready-made conceptions which thought employs in its daily operations can be of any use. Nothing is more easy than to say that the ego is multiplicity, or that it is unity, or that it is the synthesis of both. Unity and multiplicity are here representations that we have no need to cut out on the model of the object; they are found ready-made, and have only to be chosen from a heap. They are stock-size clothes which do just as well for Peter as for Paul, for they set off the form of neither. But an empiricism worthy of the name, an empiricism which works only to measure, is obliged for each new object that it studies to make an absolutely fresh effort. It cuts out for the object a concept which is appropriate to that object alone, a concept which can as yet hardly be called a concept, since it applies to this one thing. It does not proceed by combining current ideas like unity and multiplicity; but it leads us, on the contrary, to a simple, unique representation, which, however once formed, enables us to understand easily how it is that we can place it in the frames unity, multiplicity, etc., all much larger than itself. In short, philosophy thus defined does not consist in the choice of certain concepts, and in taking sides with a school, but in the search for a unique intuition from which we can descend with equal ease to different concepts, because we are placed above the divisions of the schools.

That personality has unity cannot be denied; but such an affirmation teaches one nothing about the extraordinary nature of the particular unity presented by personality. That our self is multiple I also agree, but then it must be understood that it is a multiplicity which has nothing in common with any other multiplicity. What is really important for philosophy is to know exactly what unity, what multiplicity, and what reality superior both to abstract unity and multiplicity the multiple unity of the self actually is. Now philosophy will know this only when it recovers possession of the simple intuition of the self by the self. Then, according to the direction it chooses for its descent from this summit, it will arrive at unity or multiplicity, or at any one of the concepts by which we try to define the moving life of the self. But no mingling of these concepts would give anything which at all resembles the self that endures.

If we are shown a solid cone, we see without any difficulty how it narrows towards the summit and tends to be lost in a mathematical point, and also how it enlarges in the direction of the base into an indefinitely increasing circle. But neither the point nor the circle, nor the juxtaposition of the two on a plane, would give us the least idea of a cone. The same thing holds true of the unity and multiplicity of mental life, and of the zero and the infinite towards which empiricism and rationalism conduct personality.

Concepts, as we shall show elsewhere, generally go together in couples and represent two contraries. There is hardly any concrete reality which cannot be observed from two opposing standpoints, which cannot consequently be subsumed under two antagonistic concepts. Hence a thesis and an antithesis which we endeavor in vain to reconcile logically, for the very simple reason that it is impossible, with concepts and observations taken from outside points of view, to make a thing. But from the object, seized by intuition, we pass easily in many cases to the two contrary concepts; and as in that way thesis and antithesis can be seen to spring from reality, we grasp at the same time how it is that the two are opposed and how they are reconciled.

It is true that to accomplish this, it is necessary to proceed by a reversal of the usual work of the intellect. *Thinking* usually consists in passing from concepts to things, and not from things to concepts. To know a reality, in the usual sense of the word "know," is to take ready-made concepts, to portion them out and to mix them together until a practical equivalent of the reality is obtained. But it must be remembered that the normal work of the intellect is far from being disinterested. We do not aim generally at knowledge for the sake of knowledge, but in order to take sides, to draw profit—in short, to satisfy an interest. We inquire up to what point the object we seek to know is *this* or *that*, to what known class it belongs, and what kind of action, bearing, or attitude it should suggest to us. These different possible actions and attitudes are so many *conceptual directions* of our thought, determined once for all; it remains only to follow them: in that precisely consists the application of concepts to things. To try to fit a concept on an object is simply to ask what we can do with the object, and what it can do for us. To label an object with a certain concept is to mark in precise terms the kind of action or attitude the object should suggest to us. All knowledge, properly so called, is then oriented in a certain direction, or taken from a certain point of view. It is true that our interest is often complex. This is why it happens that our knowledge of the same object may face several successive directions and may be taken from various points of view. It is this which constitutes, in the usual meaning of the terms, a "broad" and "comprehensive" knowledge of the object; the object is then brought not under one single concept, but under several in which it is supposed to "participate." How does it participate in all these concepts at the same time? This is a question which does not concern our practical action and about which we need not trouble. It is, therefore, natural and legitimate in daily life to proceed by the juxtaposition and portioning out of concepts; no philosophical difficulty will arise from this procedure, since by a tacit agreement we shall abstain from philosophizing. But to carry this *modus operandi* into philosophy, to pass here also from concepts to the thing, to use in order to obtain a disinterested knowledge of an object (that this time we desire to grasp as it is in itself) a manner of knowing inspired by a determinate interest, consisting by definition in an externally-taken view of the object, is to go against the end that we have chosen, to condemn philosophy to an eternal skirmishing between the schools and to install contradiction in the very heart of the object and of the method. Either there is no philosophy possible, and all knowledge of things is a practical knowledge aimed at the profit to be drawn from them, or else philosophy consists in placing oneself within the object itself by an effort of intuition.

But in order to understand the nature of this intuition, in order to fix with precision where intuition ends and where analysis begins, it is necessary to return to what was said earlier about the flux of duration.

It will be noted that an essential characteristic of the concepts and diagrams to which analysis leads is that, while being considered, they remain stationary. I isolate from the totality of interior life that psychical entity which I call a simple sensation. So long as I study it, I suppose that it remains constant. If I noticed any change in it, I should say that it was not a single sensation but several successive sensations, and I should then transfer to each of these successive sensations the immutability that I first attributed to the total sensation. In any case I can, by pushing the analysis far enough, always manage to arrive at elements which I agree to consider immutable. There, and there only, shall I find the solid basis of operations which science needs for its own proper development.

But, then, I cannot escape the objection that there is no state of mind, however simple, which does not change every moment, since there is no consciousness without memory, and no continuation of a state without the addition, to the present feeling, of the memory of past moments. It is this which constitutes duration. Inner duration is the continuous life of a memory which prolongs the past into the present, the present either containing within it in a distinct form the ceaselessly growing image of the past, or, more probably, showing by its continual change of quality the heavier and still heavier load we drag behind us as we grow older. Without this survival of the past into the present there would be no duration, but only instantaneity.

Probably if I am thus accused of taking the mental state out of duration by the mere fact that I analyze it, I shall reply, "Is not each of these elementary psychical states, to which my analysis leads, itself a state which occupies time? My analysis,"

I shall say, "does indeed resolve the inner life into states, each of which is homogeneous with itself; only, since the homogeneity extends over a definite number of minutes or of seconds, the elementary psychical state does not cease to endure, although it does not change."

But, in saying that, I fail to see that the definite number of minutes and of seconds, which I am attributing here to the elementary psychical state, has simply the value of a sign intended to remind me that the psychical state, supposed homogeneous, is in reality a state which changes and endures. The state, taken in itself, is a perpetual becoming. I have extracted from this becoming a certain average of quality, which I have supposed invariable; I have in this way constituted a stable and consequently schematic state. I have, on the other hand, extracted from it Becoming in general, i.e., a becoming which is not the becoming of any particular thing, and this is what I have called the *time* the state occupies. Were I to look at it closely, I should see that this abstract time is as immobile for me as the state which I localize in it, that it could flow only by a continual change of quality, and that if it is without quality, merely the theater of the change, it thus becomes an immobile medium. I should see that the construction of this homogeneous time is simply designed to facilitate the comparison between the different concrete durations, to permit us to count simultaneities, and to measure one flux of duration in relation to another. And lastly I should understand that, in attaching the sign of a definite number of minutes and of seconds to the representation of an elementary psychical state, I am merely reminding myself and others that the state has been detached from an ego which endures, and merely marking out the place where it must again be set in movement in order to bring it back from the abstract schematic thing it has become to the concrete state it was at first. But I ignore all that, because it has nothing to do with analysis.

This means that analysis operates always on the immobile, whilst intuition places itself in mobility, or, what comes to the same thing, in duration. There lies the very distinct line of demarcation between intuition and analysis. The real, the experienced, and the concrete are recognized by the fact that they are variability itself; the element by the fact that it is invariable. And the element is invariable by definition, being a diagram, a simplified reconstruction, often a mere symbol, in any case a motionless view of the moving reality.

But the error consists in believing that we can reconstruct the real with these diagrams. As we have already said and may as well repeat here—from intuition one can pass to analysis, but not from analysis to intuition.

Out of variability we can make as many variations, qualities, and modifications as we please, since these are so many static views, taken by analysis, of the mobility given to intuition. But these modifications, put end to end, will produce nothing which resembles variability, since they are not parts of it, but elements, which is quite a different thing.

Consider, for example, the variability which is nearest to homogeneity, that of movement in space. Along the whole of this movement we can imagine possible stoppages; these are what we call the positions of the moving body, or the points by which it passes. But with these positions, even with an infinite number of them, we shall never make movement. They are not parts of the movement, they are so many snapshots of it; they are, one might say, only supposed stopping-places. The moving body is never really *in* any of the points; the most we can say is that it passes through them. But passage, which is movement, has nothing in common with stoppage, which is immobility. A movement cannot be superposed on an immobility, or it would then coincide with it, which would be a contradiction. The points are not *in* the movement, as parts, nor even *beneath* it, as positions occupied by the moving body. They are simply projected by us under the movement, as so many places where a moving body, which by hypothesis does not stop, would be if it were to stop. They are not, therefore, properly speaking, positions, but "suppositions," aspects, or points of view of the mind. But how could we construct a thing with points of view?

Nevertheless, this is what we try to do whenever we reason about movement, and also about time, for which movement serves as a means of representation. As a result of an illusion deeply rooted in our mind, and because we cannot prevent ourselves from considering analysis as the equivalent of intuition, we begin by distinguishing along the whole extent of the movement a certain number of possible stoppages or points, which we make, whether they like it or no, parts of the movement. Faced with our impotence to reconstruct the movement with these points, we insert other points, believing that we can in this way get nearer to the essential mobility in the movement. Then, as this mobility still escapes us, we substitute for a fixed and finite number of points an "indefinitely increasing" number—thus vainly trying to counterfeit, by the movement of a thought that goes on indefinitely adding points to points, the real and undivided motion of the moving body. Finally, we say that movement is composed of points, but that it comprises, in addition, the obscure and mysterious passage from one position to the next. As if the obscurity was not due entirely to the fact that we have supposed immobility to be clearer than mobility and rest anterior to movement! As if the mystery did not follow entirely from our attempting to pass from stoppages to movement by way of addition, which is impossible, when it is so easy to pass, by simple diminution, from movement to the slackening of movement, and so to immobility! It is movement that we must accustom ourselves to look upon as simplest and clearest, immobility being only the extreme limit of the slowing down of movement, a limit reached only, perhaps, in thought and never realized in nature. What we have done is to seek for the meaning of the poem in the form of the letters of which it is composed; we have believed that by considering an increasing number of letters we would grasp at last the ever-escaping meaning, and in desperation, seeing that it was useless to seek for a part of the sense in each of the letters, we have supposed that it was between each letter and the next that this long-sought fragment of the mysterious sense was lodged! But the letters, it must be pointed

out once again, are not parts of the thing, but elements of the
symbol. Again, the positions of the moving body are not parts
of the movement; they are points of the space which is supposed to underlie the movement. This empty and immobile
space which is merely conceived, never perceived, has the value
of a symbol only. How could you ever manufacture reality by
manipulating symbols?

But the symbol in this case responds to the most inveterate
habits of our thought. We place ourselves as a rule in immobility, in which we find a point of support for practical purposes, and with this immobility we try to reconstruct motion.
We only obtain in this way a clumsy imitation, a counterfeit
of real movement, but this imitation is much more useful in
life than the intuition of the thing itself would be. Now our
mind has an irresistible tendency to consider that idea clearest
which is most often useful to it. That is why immobility seems
to it clearer than mobility, and rest anterior to movement.

The difficulties to which the problem of movement has
given rise from the earliest antiquity have originated in this
way. They result always from the fact that we insist on passing
from space to movement, from the trajectory to the flight,
from immobile positions to mobility, and on passing from one
to the other by way of addition. But it is movement which is
anterior to immobility, and the relation between positions and
a displacement is not that of parts to a whole, but that of the
diversity of possible points of view to the real indivisibility of
the object.

Many other problems are born of the same illusion. What
stationary points are to the movement of a moving body, concepts of different qualities are to the qualitative change of an
object. The various concepts into which a change can be analyzed are therefore so many stable views of the instability of
the real. And to think of an object—in the usual meaning of
the word "think"—is to take one or more of these immobile
views of its mobility. It consists, in short, in asking from time
to time where the object is, in order that we may know what
to do with it. Nothing could be more legitimate, moreover,

than this method of procedure, so long as we are concerned only with a practical knowledge of reality. Knowledge, in so far as it is directed to practical matters, has only to enumerate the principal possible attitudes of the thing towards us, as well as our best possible attitude towards it. Therein lies the ordinary function of ready-made concepts, those stations with which we mark out the path of becoming. But to seek to penetrate with them into the inmost nature of things, is to apply to the mobility of the real a method created in order to give stationary points of observation on it. It is to forget that, if metaphysics is possible, it can only be a laborious, and even painful, effort to remount the natural slope of the work of thought, in order to place oneself directly, by a kind of intellectual expansion, within the thing studied: in short, a passage from reality to concepts and no longer from concepts to reality. Is it astonishing that, like children trying to catch smoke by closing their hands, philosophers so often see the object they would grasp fly before them? It is in this way that many of the quarrels between the schools are perpetuated, each of them reproaching the others with having allowed the real to slip away.

But if metaphysics is to proceed by intuition, if intuition has the mobility of duration as its object, and if duration is of a psychical nature, shall we not be confining the philosopher to the exclusive contemplation of himself? Will not philosophy come to consist in watching oneself merely live, "as a sleepy shepherd watches the water flow"? [1] To talk in this way would be to return to the error which, since the beginning of this study, we have not ceased to point out. It would be to misconceive the singular nature of duration, and at the same time the essentially active, I might almost say violent, character of metaphysical intuition. It would be failing to see that the method we speak of alone permits us to go beyond idealism, as well as realism, to affirm the existence of objects inferior and superior (though in a certain sense interior) to us, to

[1] "Comme un pâtre assoupi regarde l'eau couler."—*Rolla*, Alfred de Musset. (Translator's note.)

make them coexist together without difficulty, and to dissi-
pate gradually the obscurities that analysis accumulates round
these great problems. Without entering here upon the study
of these different points, let us confine ourselves to showing
how the intuition we speak of is not a single act, but an indefinite series of acts, all doubtless of the same kind, but each
of a very particular species, and how this diversity of acts corresponds to all the degrees of being.

If I seek to *analyze* duration—that is, to resolve it into ready-
made concepts—I am compelled, by the very nature of the
concepts and of analysis, to take two opposing views of *duration in general,* with which I then attempt to reconstruct it.
This combination, which will have, moreover, something mi-
raculous about it—since one does not understand how two
contraries would ever meet each other—can present neither a
diversity of degrees nor a variety of forms; like all miracles, it
is or it is not. I shall have to say, for example, that there is, on
the one hand, a *multiplicity* of successive states of consciousness, and, on the other, a *unity* which binds them together.
Duration will be the "synthesis" of this unity and this multiplicity, a mysterious operation which takes place in darkness,
and in regard to which, I repeat, one does not see how it
would admit of shades or of degrees. In this hypothesis there
is, and can only be, one single duration, that in which our
own consciousness habitually works. To express it more clearly
—if we consider duration under the simple aspect of a movement accomplishing itself in space, and we seek to reduce to
concepts movement considered as representative of time, we
shall have, on the one hand, as great a number of points on
the trajectory as we may desire, and, on the other hand, an
abstract unity which holds them together as a thread holds
together the pearls of a necklace. Between this abstract multiplicity and this abstract unity, the combination, when once
it has been posited as possible, is something unique, which
will no more admit of shades than does the addition of given
numbers in arithmetic. But if, instead of professing to analyze
duration (i.e., at bottom, to make a synthesis of it with con-

cepts), we at once place ourselves in it by an effort of intuition, we have the feeling of a certain very determinate tension, in which the determination itself appears as a choice between an infinity of possible durations. Henceforward we can picture to ourselves as many durations as we wish, all very different from each other, although each of them, on being reduced to concepts—that is, observed externally from two opposing points of view—always comes in the end to the same indefinable combination of the many and the one.

Let us express the same idea with more precision. If I consider duration as a multiplicity of moments bound to each other by a unity which goes through them like a thread, then, however short the chosen duration may be, these moments are unlimited in number. I can suppose them as close together as I please; there will always be between these mathematical points other mathematical points, and so on to infinity. Looked at from the point of view of multiplicity, then, duration disintegrates into a powder of moments, none of which endures, each being an instantaneity. If, on the other hand, I consider the unity which binds the moments together, this cannot endure either, since by hypothesis everything that is changing, and everything that is really durable in the duration, has been put to the account of the multiplicity of moments. As I probe more deeply into its essence, this unity will appear to me as some immobile substratum of that which is moving, as some intemporal essence of time; it is this that I shall call eternity; an eternity of death, since it is nothing else than the movement emptied of the mobility which made its life. Closely examined, the opinions of the opposing schools on the subject of duration would be seen to differ solely in this, that they attribute a capital importance to one or the other of these two concepts. Some adhere to the point of view of the multiple; they set up as concrete reality the distinct moments of a time which they have reduced to powder; the unity which enables us to call the grains a powder they hold to be much more artificial. Others, on the contrary, set up the unity of duration as concrete reality. They place themselves in the eternal. But as their eternity remains, notwithstanding, abstract, since it is empty, being the eternity of a concept which, by hypothesis, excludes from itself the opposing concept, one does not see how this eternity would permit of an indefinite number of moments coexisting in it. In the first hypothesis we have a world resting on nothing, which must end and begin again of its own accord at each instant. In the second we have an infinity of abstract eternity, about which also it is just as difficult to understand why it does not remain enveloped in itself and how it allows things to coexist with it. But in both cases, and whichever of the two metaphysics it be that one is switched into, time appears, from the psychological point of view, as a mixture of two abstractions, which admit of neither degrees nor shades. In one system as in the other, there is only one unique duration, which carries everything with it—a bottomless, bankless river, which flows without assignable force in a direction which could not be defined. Even then we can call it only a river, and the river only flows, because reality obtains from the two doctrines this concession, profiting by a moment of perplexity in their logic. As soon as they recover from this perplexity, they freeze this flux either into an immense solid sheet, or into an infinity of crystallized needles, always into a *thing* which necessarily partakes of the immobility of a *point of view*.

It is quite otherwise if we place ourselves from the first, by an effort of intuition, in the concrete flow of duration. Certainly, we shall then find no logical reason for positing multiple and diverse durations. Strictly, there might well be no other duration than our own, as, for example, there might be no other color in the world but orange. But just as a consciousness based on color, which sympathized internally with orange instead of perceiving it externally, would feel itself held between red and yellow, would even perhaps suspect beyond this last color a complete spectrum into which the continuity from red to yellow might expand naturally, so the intuition of our duration, far from leaving us suspended in the void as pure analysis would do, brings us into contact with a whole continuity of durations which we must try to follow, whether downwards or upwards; in both cases we can extend ourselves indefinitely by an increasingly violent effort, in both cases we transcend ourselves. In the first we advance towards a more and more attenuated duration, the pulsations of which, being more rapid than ours, and dividing our simple sensation, dilute its quality into quantity; at the limit would be pure homogeneity, that pure *repetition* by which we define materiality. Advancing in the other direction, we approach a duration which *strains*, contracts, and intensifies itself more and more; at the limit would be eternity. No longer conceptual eternity, which is an eternity of death, but an eternity of life. A living and therefore still moving eternity in which our own particular duration would be included as the vibrations are in light; an eternity which would be the concentration of all duration, as materiality is its dispersion. Between these two extreme limits intuition moves, and this movement is the very essence of metaphysics.

*

*   *

There can be no question of following here the various stages of this movement. But having presented a general view of the method and made a first application of it, it may not be amiss to formulate, as precisely as we can, the principles on which it rests. Most of the following propositions have already received in this essay some degree of proof. We hope to demonstrate them more completely when we come to deal with other problems.

I. *There is a reality that is external and yet given immediately to the mind.* Common sense is right on this point, as against the idealism and realism of the philosophers.

II. This reality is mobility. Not *things* made, but things in the making, not self-maintaining *states*, but only changing states, exist. Rest is never more than apparent, or, rather, relative. The consciousness we have of our own self in its continual flux introduces us to the interior of a reality, on the model of which we must represent other realities. *All reality, therefore, is tendency, if we agree to mean by tendency an incipient change of direction.*

III. Our mind, which seeks for solid points of support, has for its main function in the ordinary course of life that of representing *states* and *things*. It takes, at long intervals, almost instantaneous views of the undivided mobility of the real. It thus obtains *sensations* and *ideas*. In this way it substitutes for the continuous the discontinuous, for motion stability, for tendency in process of change, fixed points marking a direction of change and tendency. This substitution is necessary to common sense, to language, to practical life, and even, in a certain sense, which we shall endeavor to determine, to positive science. *Our intellect, when it follows its natural bent, proceeds, on the one hand, by solid perceptions, and, on the other, by stable conceptions.* It starts from the immobile, and only conceives and expresses movement as a function of immobility. It takes up its position in ready-made concepts, and endeavors to catch in them, as in a net, something of the reality which passes. This is certainly not done in order to obtain an internal and metaphysical knowledge of the real, but simply in order to utilize the real, each concept (as also each sensation) being a *practical question* which our activity puts to reality and to which reality replies, as must be done in business, by a Yes or a No. But, in doing that, it lets that which is its very essence escape from the real.

IV. The inherent difficulties of metaphysics, the antinomies which it gives rise to, and the contradictions into which it falls, the division into antagonistic schools, and the irreducible opposition between systems are largely the result of our applying, to the disinterested knowledge of the real, processes which we generally employ for practical ends. They arise from the fact that we place ourselves in the immobile in order to lie in wait for the moving thing as it passes, instead of replacing ourselves in the moving thing itself, in order to traverse with it the immobile positions. They arise from our professing to reconstruct reality—which is tendency and consequently mobility—with percepts and concepts whose function it is to make it stationary. With stoppages, however numerous they may be, we shall never make mobility; whereas, if mobility is given, we can, by means of diminution, obtain from it by thought as many stoppages as we desire. In other words, *it is clear that fixed concepts may be extracted by our thought from mobile reality; but there are no means of reconstructing the mobility of the real with fixed concepts.* Dogmatism, however, in so far as it has been a builder of systems, has always attempted this reconstruction.

V. In this it was bound to fail. It is on this impotence and on this impotence only that the skeptical, idealist, critical doctrines really dwell: in fact, all doctrines that deny to our intelligence the power of attaining the absolute. But because we fail to reconstruct the living reality with stiff and ready-made concepts, it does not follow that we cannot grasp it in some other way. *The demonstrations which have been given of the relativity of our knowledge are therefore tainted with an original vice; they imply, like the dogmatism they attack, that all knowledge must necessarily start from concepts with fixed outlines, in order to clasp with them the reality which flows.*

VI. But the truth is that our intelligence can follow the opposite method. It can place itself within the mobile reality, and adopt its ceaselessly changing direction; in short, can grasp it by means of that *intellectual sympathy* which we call intuition. This is extremely difficult. The mind has to do violence to itself, has to reverse the direction of the operation by which it habitually thinks, has perpetually to revise, or rather to recast, all its categories. But in this way it will attain to fluid concepts, capable of following reality in all its sinuosities and of adopting the very movement of the inward life of things. Only thus will a progressive philosophy be built up, freed from the disputes which arise between the various schools, and able to solve its problems naturally, because it will be released from the artificial expression in terms of which such problems are posited. *To philosophize, therefore, is to invert the habitual direction of the work of thought.*

VII. This inversion has never been practiced in a methodical manner; but a profoundly considered history of human thought would show that we owe to it all that is greatest in the sciences, as well as all that is permanent in metaphysics. The most powerful of the methods of investigation at the disposal of the human mind, the infinitesimal calculus, originated from this very inversion. Modern mathematics is precisely an effort to substitute the *being made* for the *ready-made,* to follow the generation of magnitudes, to grasp motion no longer from without and in its displayed result, but from within and in its tendency to change; in short, to adopt the mobile continuity of the outlines of things. It is true that it is confined to the outline, being only the science of magnitudes. It is true also that it has only been able to achieve its marvelous applications by the invention of certain symbols, and that if the intuition of which we have just spoken lies at the origin of invention, it is the symbol alone which is concerned in the application. But metaphysics, which aims at no application, can and usually must abstain from converting intuition into symbols. Liberated from the obligation of working for practically useful results, it will indefinitely enlarge the domain of its investigations. What it may lose in comparison with science in utility and exactitude, it will regain in range and extension. Though mathematics is only the science of magnitudes, though mathematical processes are applicable only to quantities, it must not be forgotten that quantity is always quality in a nascent state; it is, we might say, the limiting case of equality. It is natural, then, that metaphysics should adopt the generative idea of our mathematics in order to extend it to all qualities; that is, to reality in general. It will not, by doing this, in any way be moving towards universal mathematics, that chimera of modern philosophy. On the contrary, the farther it goes, the more untranslatable into symbols will be the objects it encounters. But it will at least have begun by getting into contact with the continuity and mobility of the real, just where this contact can be most marvelously utilized. It will have contemplated itself in a mirror which reflects an image of itself, much shrunken, no doubt, but for that reason very luminous. It will have seen with greater clearness what the mathematical processes borrow from concrete reality, and it will continue in the direction of concrete reality, and not in that of mathematical processes. Having then discounted beforehand what is too modest, and at the same time too ambitious, in the following formula, we may say that *the object of metaphysics is to perform* qualitative *differentiations and integrations.*

VIII. The reason why this object has been lost sight of, and why science itself has been mistaken in the origin of the processes it employs, is that intuition, once attained, must find a mode of expression and of application which conforms to the habits of our thought, and one which furnishes us, in the shape of well-defined concepts, with the solid points of support which we so greatly need. In that lies the condition of what we call exactitude and precision, and also the condition of the unlimited extension of a general method to particular cases. Now this extension and this work of logical improvement can be continued for centuries, whilst the act which creates the method lasts but for a moment. That is why we so often take the logical equipment of science for science itself,[2] forgetting the metaphysical intuition from which all the rest has sprung.

From the overlooking of this intuition proceeds all that has been said by philosophers and by men of science themselves about the "relativity" of scientific knowledge. *What is relative is the symbolic knowledge by pre-existing concepts, which proceeds from the fixed to the moving, and not the intuitive knowledge which installs itself in that which is moving and adopts the very life of things.* This intuition attains the absolute.

Science and metaphysics therefore come together in intu-

2 On this point as on several other questions treated in the present essay, see the interesting articles by MM. Le Roy, Vincent, and Wilbois, which have appeared in the *Revue de Métaphysique et de Morale.*

ition. A truly intuitive philosophy would realize the much-desired union of science and metaphysics. While it would make of metaphysics a positive science—that is, a progressive and indefinitely perfectible one—it would at the same time lead the positive sciences, properly so called, to become conscious of their true scope, often far greater than they imagine. It would put more science into metaphysics, and more metaphysics into science. It would result in restoring the continuity between the intuitions which the various sciences have obtained here and there in the course of their history, and which they have obtained only by strokes of genius.

IX. That there are not two different ways of knowing things fundamentally, that the various sciences have their root in metaphysics, is what the ancient philosophers generally thought. Their error did not lie there. It consisted in their being always dominated by the belief, so natural to the human mind, that a variation can only be the expression and development of what is invariable. Whence it followed that action was an enfeebled contemplation, duration a deceptive and shifting image of immobile eternity, the Soul a fall from the Idea. The whole of the philosophy which begins with Plato and culminates in Plotinus is the development of a principle which may be formulated thus: "There is more in the immutable than in the moving, and we pass from the stable to the unstable by a mere diminution." Now it is the contrary which is true.

Modern science dates from the day when mobility was set up as an independent reality. It dates from the day when Galileo, setting a ball rolling down an inclined plane, firmly resolved to study this movement from top to bottom for itself, in itself, instead of seeking its principle in the concepts of *high* and *low*, two immobilities by which Aristotle believed he could adequately explain the mobility. And this is not an isolated fact in the history of science. Several of the great discoveries, of those at least which have transformed the positive sciences or which have created new ones, have been so many soundings in the depths of pure duration. The more living the reality touched, the deeper was the sounding.

But the lead-line sunk to the sea bottom brings up a fluid mass which the sun's heat quickly dries into solid and discontinuous grains of sand. And the intuition of duration, when it is exposed to the rays of the understanding, in like manner quickly turns into fixed, distinct, and immobile concepts. In the living mobility of things the understanding is bent on marking real or virtual stations, it notes departures and arrivals; for this is all that concerns the thought of man in so far as it is simply human. It is more than human to grasp what is happening in the interval. But philosophy can only be an effort to transcend the human condition.

Men of science have fixed their attention mainly on the concepts with which they have marked out the pathway of intuition. The more they laid stress on these residual products, which have turned into symbols, the more they attributed a symbolic character to every kind of science. And the more they believed in the symbolic character of science, the more did they indeed make science symbolical. Gradually they have blotted out all difference, in positive science, between the natural and the artificial, between the data of immediate intuition, and the enormous work of analysis which the understanding pursues round intuition. Thus they have prepared the way for a doctrine which affirms the relativity of all our knowledge.

But metaphysics has also labored to the same end.

How could the masters of modern philosophy, who have been renovators of science as well as of metaphysics, have had no sense of the moving continuity of reality? How could they have abstained from placing themselves in what we call concrete duration? They have done so to a greater extent than they were aware; above all, much more than they said. If we endeavor to link together, by a continuous connection, the intuitions about which systems have become organized, we find, together with other convergent and divergent lines, one very determinate direction of thought and of feeling. What is this latent thought? How shall we express the feeling? To borrow once more the language of the Platonists, we will say—depriving the words of their psychological sense, and giving the name of Idea to a certain settling down into easy intelligibility, and that of Soul to a certain longing after the restlessness of life—that an invisible current causes modern philosophy to place the Soul above the Idea. It thus tends, like modern science, and even more so than modern science, to advance in an opposite direction to ancient thought.

But this metaphysics, like this science, has enfolded its deeper life in a rich tissue of symbols, forgetting sometimes that, while science needs symbols for its analytical development, the main object of metaphysics is to do away with symbols. Here, again, the understanding has pursued its work of fixing, dividing, and reconstructing. It has pursued this, it is true, under a rather different form. Without insisting on a point which we propose to develop elsewhere, it is enough here to say that the understanding, whose function it is to operate on stable elements, may look for stability either in *relations* or in *things*. In so far as it works on concepts of relations, it culminates in *scientific* symbolism. In so far as it works on concepts of things, it culminates in *metaphysical* symbolism. But in both cases the arrangement comes from the understanding. Hence, it would fain believe itself independent. Rather than recognize at once what it owes to an intuition of the depths of reality, it prefers exposing itself to the danger that its whole work may be looked upon as nothing but an artificial arrangement of symbols. So that if we were to hold on to the letter of what metaphysicians and scientists say, and also to the material aspect of what they do, we might believe that the metaphysicians have dug a deep tunnel beneath reality, that the scientists have thrown an elegant bridge over it, but that the moving stream of things passes between these two artificial constructions without touching them.

One of the principal artifices of the Kantian criticism consisted in taking the metaphysician and the scientist literally, forcing both metaphysics and science to the extreme limit of symbolism to which they could go, and to which, moreover, they make their way of their own accord as soon as the understanding claims an independence full of perils. Having once overlooked the ties that bind science and metaphysics to intellectual intuition, Kant has no difficulty in showing that our science is wholly relative, and our metaphysics entirely artificial. Since he has exaggerated the independence of the understanding in both cases, since he has relieved both metaphysics and science of the intellectual intuition which served them as inward ballast, science with its relations presents to him no more than a film of form, and metaphysics, with its things, no more than a film of matter. Is it surprising that the first, then, reveals to him only frames packed within frames, and the second only phantoms chasing phantoms?

He has struck such telling blows at our science and our metaphysics that they have not even yet quite recovered from their bewilderment. Our mind would readily resign itself to seeing in science a knowledge that is wholly relative, and in metaphysics a speculation that is entirely empty. It seems to us, even at this present date, that the Kantian criticism applies to all metaphysics and to all science. In reality, it applies more especially to the philosophy of the ancients, as also to the form—itself borrowed from the ancients—in which the moderns have most often left their thought. It is valid against a metaphysics which claims to give us a *single* and completed system of things, against a science professing to be a *single* system of relations; in short, against a science and a metaphysics presenting themselves with the architectural simplicity of the Platonic theory of ideas or of a Greek temple. If metaphysics claims to be made up of concepts which were ours before its advent, if it consists in an ingenious arrangement of pre-existing ideas which we utilize as building material for an edifice, if, in short, it is anything else but the constant expansion of our mind, the ever-renewed effort to transcend our actual ideas and perhaps also our elementary logic, it is but too evident that, like all the works of pure understanding, it becomes artificial. And if science is wholly and entirely a work of analysis or of conceptual representation, if experience is only to serve therein as a verification for "clear ideas," if, instead of starting from multiple and diverse intuition—which insert themselves in the particular movement of each reality, but do not always dovetail into each other—it professes to be a vast mathematics, a single and closed-in system of relations, imprisoning the whole of reality in a network prepared in advance—it becomes a knowledge purely relative to human understanding. If we look carefully into the *Critique of Pure Reason,* we see that science for Kant did indeed mean this kind of *universal mathematics,* and metaphysics this practically unaltered *Platonism.* In truth, the dream of a universal mathematics is itself but a survival of Platonism. Universal mathematics is what the world of ideas becomes when we suppose that the Idea consists in a relation or in a law, and no longer in a thing. Kant [3] took this dream of a few modern philosophers for a reality; more than this, he believed that all scientific knowledge was only a detached fragment of, or rather a steppingstone to, universal mathematics. Hence the main task of the *Critique* was to lay the foundation of this mathematics—that is, to determine what the intellect must be, and what the object, in order that an uninterrupted mathematics may bind them together. And of necessity, if all possible experience can be made to enter thus into the rigid and already formed framework of our understanding, it is (unless we assume a pre-established harmony) because our understanding itself organizes nature, and finds itself again therein as in a mirror. Hence the possibility of science, which owes all its efficacy to its relativity, and the impossibility of metaphysics, since the latter finds nothing more to do than to parody with phantoms of things the work of conceptual arrangement which science practices seriously on relations. Briefly, *the whole* Critique of Pure Reason *ends in establishing that Platonism, illegitimate if Ideas are things, becomes legitimate if Ideas are relations, and that the ready-made idea, once brought down in this way from heaven to earth, is in fact,*

---

[3] See on this subject a very interesting article by Radulescu-Motru, 'Zur Entwicklung von Kants Theorie der Naturcausalität," in Wundt's *Philosophische Studien* (Vol. IX, 1894).

as Plato held, the common basis alike of thought and of nature. But the whole of the Critique of Pure Reason *also rests on this postulate, that our intellect is incapable of anything but Platonizing*—that is, of pouring all possible experience into pre-existing molds.

On this the whole question depends. If scientific knowledge is indeed what Kant supposed, then there is one simple science, preformed and even preformulated in nature, as Aristotle believed; great discoveries, then, serve only to illuminate, point by point, the already drawn line of this logic, immanent in things, just as on the night of a fete we light up one by one the rows of gas-jets which already outline the shape of some building. And if metaphysical knowledge is really what Kant supposed, it is reduced to a *choice* between two attitudes of the mind before all the great problems, both equally possible; its manifestations are so many arbitrary and always ephemeral choices between two solutions, virtually formulated from all eternity: it lives and dies by antinomies. But the truth is that modern science does not present this unilinear simplicity, nor does modern metaphysics these irreducible oppositions.

Modern science is neither one nor simple. It rests, I freely admit, on ideas which in the end we find clear; but these ideas have gradually become clear through the use made of them; they owe most of their clearness to the light which the facts, and the applications to which they led, have by reflection shed on them—the clearness of a concept being scarcely anything more at bottom than the certainty, at last obtained, of manipulating the concept profitably. At its origin, more than one of these concepts must have appeared obscure, not easily reconcilable with the concepts already admitted into science, and indeed very near the borderline of absurdity. This means that science does not proceed by an orderly dovetailing together of concepts predestined to fit each other exactly. True and fruitful ideas are so many close contacts with currents of reality, which do not necessarily converge on the same point. However, the concepts in which they lodge themselves manage somehow, by rubbing off each other's corners, to settle down well enough together.

On the other hand, modern metaphysics is not made up of solutions so radical that they can culminate in irreducible oppositions. It would be so, no doubt, if there were no means of accepting at the same time and on the same level the thesis and the antithesis of the antinomies. But philosophy consists precisely in this, that by an effort of intuition one places oneself within that concrete reality, of which the *Critique* takes from without the two opposed views, thesis and antithesis. I could never imagine how black and white interpenetrate if I had never seen gray; but once I have seen gray I easily understand how it can be considered from two points of view, that of white and that of black. Doctrines which have a certain basis of intuition escape the Kantian criticism exactly in so far as they are intuitive; and these doctrines are the whole of metaphysics, provided we ignore the metaphysics which is fixed and dead in *theses,* and consider only that which is living in *philosophers.* The divergencies between the schools—that is, broadly speaking, between the groups of disciples formed round a few great masters—are certainly striking. But would we find them as marked between the masters themselves? Something here dominates the diversity of systems, something, we repeat, which is simple and definite like a sounding, about which one feels that it has touched at greater or less depth the bottom of the same ocean, though each time it brings up to the surface very different materials. It is on these materials that the disciples usually work; in this lies the function of analysis. And the master, in so far as he formulates, develops, and translates into abstract ideas what he brings, is already in a way his own disciple. But the simple act which started the analysis, and which conceals itself behind the analysis, proceeds from a faculty quite different from the analytical. This is, by its very definition, intuition.

In conclusion, we may remark that there is nothing mysterious in this faculty. Every one of us has had occasion to exercise it to a certain extent. Any one of us, for instance, who has attempted literary composition, knows that when the subject has been studied at length, the materials all collected, and the notes all made, something more is needed in order to set about the work of composition itself, and that is an often very painful effort to place ourselves directly at the heart of the subject, and to seek as deeply as possible an impulse, after which we need only let ourselves go. This impulse, once received, starts the mind on a path where it rediscovers all the information it had collected, and a thousand other details besides; it develops and analyzes itself into terms which could be enumerated indefinitely. The farther we go, the more terms we discover; we shall never say all that could be said, and yet, if we turn back suddenly upon the impulse that we feel behind us, and try to seize it, it is gone; for it was not a thing, but the direction of a movement, and though indefinitely extensible, it is infinitely simple. Metaphysical intuition seems to be something of the same kind. What corresponds here to the documents and notes of literary composition is the sum of observations and experience gathered together by positive science. For we do not obtain an intuition from reality—that is, an intellectual sympathy with the most intimate part of it—unless we have won its confidence by a long fellowship with its superficial manifestations. And it is not merely a question of assimilating the most conspicuous facts; so immense a mass of facts must be accumulated and fused together, that in this fusion all the preconceived and premature ideas which observers may unwittingly have put into their observations will be certain to neutralize each other. In this way only can the bare materiality of the known facts be exposed to view. Even in the simple and privileged case which we have used as an example, even for the direct contact of the self with the self, the final effort of distinct intuition would be impossible to anyone who had not combined and compared with each other a very large number of psychological analyses. The masters of modern philosophy were men who had assimilated all the scientific knowledge of their time, and the partial eclipse of metaphysics for the last half-century has evidently no other cause than the extraordinary difficulty which the philosopher finds today in getting into touch with positive science, which has become far too specialized. But metaphysical intuition, although it can be obtained only through material knowledge, is quite other than the mere summary or synthesis of that knowledge. It is distinct from these, we repeat, as the motor impulse is distinct from the path traversed by the moving body, as the tension of the spring is distinct from the visible movements of the pendulum. In this sense metaphysics has nothing in common with a generalization of facts, and nevertheless it might be defined as *integral experience.*

THE END